VICTORIAN ENGLAND

With special thanks to Professor Carl B. Estabrook
of the Department of History, Dartmouth College,
Hanover, New Hampshire,
for his expert reading of the manuscript

VICTORIAN ENGLAND

RUTH ASHBY

MARSHALL CAVENDISH
NEW YORK

To Ernie

Benchmark Books
Marshall Cavendish
99 White Plains Road
Tarrytown, New York 10591-9001
www.marshallcavendish.com

Library of Congress Cataloging-in-Publication Data

Ashby, Ruth.
Victorian England / by Ruth Ashby.
p. cm. — (Cultures of the past)
Summary: Describes English society in the years of Queen Victoria's reign (1837–1901), with attention to class structure, gender roles, artistic and scientific achievements.
Includes bibliographical references (p.) and index.
ISBN 0-7614-1493-2
1. Great Britain—History—Victoria, 1837–1901—Juvenile literature. 2. England—Civilization—19th century—Juvenile literature. [1. Great Britain—History—Victoria, 1837–1901. 2. England—Civilization—19th century.] I. Title. II. Series.
DA550 .A69 2003
941.081—dc21 2002002184

Printed in Hong Kong
1 3 5 6 4 2

Book design by Carol Matsuyama
Art research by Rose Corbett Gordon, Mystic CT.

Front cover: A Family Gathering, by Joseph Clark (1834–1926)
Back cover: Reading the News, by James Tissot (1836–1902)

Photo Credits

Front cover: Fine Art Photographic Library, London/Art Resource, NY; back cover: Christie's Images, London/Bridgeman Art Library; page 7: Bradford Art Galleries and Museums, West Yorkshire/Bridgeman Art Library; pages 8, 34, 37, 51, 60, 64–65: Fine Art Photographic Library, London/Art Resource, NY; pages 10, 73: Ashmolean Museum, Oxford/Bridgeman Art Library; page 13: Giraudon/Art Resource, NY; page 15: National Trust/Art Resource, NY; pages 16–17: New Walk Museum, Leicester City Museum Service, /Bridgeman Art Library; page 19: Royal Holloway, University of London /Bridgeman Art Library; pages 20, 43, 63: Private Collection/Bridgeman Art Library; page 22: Victoria & Albert Museum/Art Resource, NY; page 24: Art Resource, NY; pages 25, 57: Tate Gallery/Art Resource, NY; pages 29, 52: North Wind Picture Archives; page 31: Guildhall Art Gallery, Corporation of London/Bridgeman Art Library; page 33: National Gallery, London/Bridgeman Art Library; pages 39, 40: The Pierpont Morgan Library/Art Resource, NY; pages 44–45: Erich Lessing/Art Resource, NY; pages 46, 59: Victoria & Albert Museum, London/Bridgeman Art Library; page 47: N. Carter/North Wind Picture Archives; page 49: Manchester City Art Galleries/Bridgeman Art Library; page 55: R.S.A., London/Bridgeman Art Library; page 67: Mary Evans Picture Library; page 68: Topham/The Image Works; page 71: Sepp Seitz/Woodfin Camp & Associates; page 72: The Granger Collection, New York.

Contents

CHAPTER ONE

A Time of Change

On the morning of June 20, 1837, young Princess Victoria was awakened at six o'clock and informed that the king was dead—and that she, Victoria, was queen of the United Kingdom of Great Britain and Ireland. Victoria recorded the occasion in her diary and added:

> *Since it has pleased Providence to place me in this station, I shall do my utmost to fulfill my duty towards my country; I am very young and perhaps in many, though not in all things, inexperienced, but I am sure, that very few have more real good will and more real desire to do what is fit and right than I have.*

Victoria's determination to do what was right would see her through the longest reign in English history. The earnest and dutiful monarch was probably the perfect person to preside over the sixty-four years of change and expansion that followed, to which she gave her name: the Victorian Age.

It was a period of ceaseless activity, dynamic change, and fertile invention. Between 1830 and 1900, people in the Western world went from letter writing to telephones, stagecoaches to automobiles, wooden sailboats to iron warships. Victorians saw advances in scientific, technological, and democratic ideas that rocked the foundations of their social, religious, and political systems. An awakening social conscience brought innovations in laws and institutions to help the poor, the sick, and the needy. In 1897, American writer Mark Twain was in London to witness the Queen's Diamond Jubilee, celebrating sixty years of rule. "British history is two thousand years old," he marveled, "and yet in a good many ways the world has moved farther ahead since the Queen was born than it moved in all the rest of the two thousand put together."

Victorians were well aware of their uniqueness. Their pride sometimes degenerated into smugness, their authority into arrogance. Yet they were far from being merely the self-satisfied, narrow-minded people their critics said they were. As a recent historian has noted, the "Victorians were engaged in a tremendously exciting adventure—the daring experiment of fitting industrial man into a democratic society. . . . The Victorians found greatness, stability, and peace and the whole world, marveling, envied them for it."

In 1837, England was on the verge of remarkable achievement.

Eighteen-year-old Victoria is crowned queen at Westminster Abbey on June 28, 1837.

An Island Kingdom

The two British Isles of Great Britain* and Ireland lie off the coast of western Europe, separated from the mainland only by the narrow English Channel and the icy North Sea. The distance between Britain and the European continent is not great—only twenty miles at the narrowest point. Yet that slender barrier made all the difference in Britain's history, keeping Europe's wars at bay and encouraging a national spirit of independence. It also made possible the development of a superb maritime defense, leading to Britain's proud claim to be Ruler of the Seas. By 1830, the English navy was the strongest in the world. It not only defended England against foreign aggression but also protected the world's most profitable overseas trading empire.

*The British Isles are made up of two large islands, Great Britain and Ireland, and numerous small ones. The island of Great Britain contains three political divisions: England, Scotland, and Wales. In the nineteenth century, the nation known as the United Kingdom was comprised of Great Britain and all of Ireland. After the creation of an independent Irish nation in southern Ireland in 1922, only Northern Ireland remained part of the United Kingdom. (Still, in everyday speech and writing, we often say England when we mean Great Britain, and Britain when we mean the United Kingdom.)

The British Royal Navy defeats Napoléon Bonaparte's French fleet at the Battle of Trafalgar on October 21, 1805. In the nineteenth century, the Royal Navy was the strongest in the world.

THE UNITED KINGDOM IN THE NINETEENTH CENTURY

Atlantic Ocean

SCOTLAND

GREAT BRITAIN

North Sea

IRELAND

Liverpool

Leeds

Manchester

WALES

Birmingham

ENGLAND

Cardiff

Oxford

London

Portsmouth

0 50 100 Miles

0 100 Kilometers

English Channel

In 1801, Parliament passed the Act of Union, officially creating the United Kingdom of Great Britain and Ireland. England had controlled Ireland since the twelfth century. But Catholic Ireland resented the rule of Protestant Great Britain. The alienation between the two countries only increased as the century went on.

When Queen Victoria ascended the throne, she joined a line of succession reaching back to Alfred the Great in the ninth century. The nation she "ruled," however, was very much a constitutional monarchy, governed in reality by Parliament, which consisted of an elected House of Commons and a hereditary House of Lords. The queen herself had limited powers, confined to advising the prime minister and using her prestige to influence both Parliament and the people.

Nonetheless, the symbolic importance of the monarchy was considerable. In 1837, the English people were overjoyed to welcome a new monarch to the throne. The rulers of the last hundred years had been neither inspiring nor, many felt, truly English. George I (1660–1727), Victoria's great-great-great-grandfather, could not even speak the language when he was called to the throne from Hanover, Germany. His great-grandson George III (1738–1820), best known for losing the American colonies in the War of Independence, spent his last years mad and alone, suffering from a hereditary psychological disease. King George IV (1762–1830), interested only in fashion, gambling, and the ladies of the court, was despised for his self-indulgent ways. His brother William IV (1765–1837) was king for merely seven years and left little mark on the country.

Then came eighteen-year-old Queen Victoria, young, fresh, and eager to serve. She signaled a new day for the monarchy, although some worried about her fitness for the job. When writer Thomas Carlyle saw her gilded coach pass by after the coronation, he sighed, "Poor little Queen, she is

A portrait miniature of Queen Victoria, 1839. Although not considered beautiful, the queen had lovely skin, big blue eyes, and tiny hands of which she was very proud.

QUEEN VICTORIA (1819–1901)

When Princess Victoria was eleven, her governess told her that she was next in line for the British throne. "I will be good," she is said to have declared. And she was—a good mother, a good wife, and a good queen. Victoria certainly had her faults. Before marrying her, Prince Albert of Saxe-Coburg-Gotha wrote that the queen was "said to be incredibly stubborn and her extreme obstinacy to be constantly at war with her good nature." But she had excellent intentions, and the firm resolve to carry them out.

The young Victoria led a sheltered life in Kensington Palace, isolated from relatives and the nobility by her vigilant mother and her governess. The strong-willed Victoria so disliked being dominated that practically her first act as queen was to banish her mother to the other end of the palace.

Luckily, Victoria found a husband to whom she could give her heart and soul. She fell in love with Prince Albert's good looks and intelligence when he came to visit from Germany (as queen, *she* had to propose to *him!*). Hardworking and morally earnest, Albert used his influence to shape his wife's reign. He tried to teach her to be above party politics (she had natural Conservative tendencies) and to be as conscientious as he was. Their happy marriage and nine children became the pride of the nation. "So unlike the home life of our own dear queen," one lady was heard to murmur during a particularly violent performance of Shakespeare's *Antony and Cleopatra.*

When Albert died in 1861 at age forty-two, the queen was devastated. She put on her black "widow's weeds" and wore mourning for the rest of her life. For years, the Widow of Windsor, as she became known, withdrew from public life. Naturally, her popularity suffered as a result.

But she remained engrossed in the welfare of her children, whom she saw married into the royal houses of Europe. And she continued to carry out her political duties. She was thrilled when, against much parliamentary opposition, Prime Minister Benjamin Disraeli passed a bill making her empress of India in 1876. She took that role seriously enough to start learning the Indian language Hindustani. And she kept two Indian servants by her at all times.

By the time of her death, Queen Victoria had already become a legend. It is generally agreed that, together with Queen Elizabeth I, Victoria was one of the two greatest English monarchs. She led no battles, discovered no new continents, masterminded no political revolutions. But Victoria stood guard over her nation at the moment of its greatest success, and her people loved her for it.

at an age at which a girl can hardly be trusted to choose a bonnet for herself; yet a task is laid upon her from which an archangel might shrink." But her fragile appearance was deceiving. Victoria was a lot tougher than she looked.

She would rule a country that was already a world power. Forty-eight years earlier, the European establishment had been rocked by the French Revolution. In 1789, rebels deposed the French king, overthrew the nobility, and attempted to establish a constitutional republic. At first, liberal Britons were thrilled by the republican movement. But even the most idealistic were horrified when the Revolution was hijacked by extremists and degenerated into bloodshed and public executions. Britain ended up going to war against the French revolutionary government and then against Napoléon Bonaparte, who tried to conquer all of Europe after seizing power in 1799. England defeated Napoléon for the final time at the Battle of Waterloo in 1815. That success enabled Britain to assume the mantle of European leadership.

For the rest of the nineteenth century, the British feared their own revolution. But it never came. Instead, Victorian Britain suffered an upheaval that proved just as transforming and traumatic as any political revolt—the Industrial Revolution.

The Workshop of the World

For nearly all of human history, practically everything was made by hand. Housewives spun thread on a spinning wheel. Weavers made cloth on a loom. Millers ground wheat at a mill, using only the raw power of water or wind. Farmers sowed crops with the help of an animal-driven plow and harvested them with a handheld reaper.

Then, in the 1700s, the world of work began to change, one machine at a time. In 1701, Jethro Tull invented a mechanical seed sower. In 1733, John Kay patented the flying shuttle, which wove thread across a loom mechanically. James Hargreaves's spinning jenny of 1764 and Samuel Crompton's mule of 1779 automated the spinning wheel. Soon there was a thriving cotton industry in the north of England, where raw cotton imported from America was turned into cloth in the first textile mills.

The biggest breakthrough came in 1769, when an ingenious Scotsman named James Watt perfected the first efficient steam engine.

A steam locomotive puffs away from a dock in the port city of Cardiff, Wales. Steam powered the Industrial Revolution in Britain—its locomotives, factories, and ships.

By the first two decades of the nineteenth century, steam was powering textile machines, mining pumps, locomotives, and steamboats. The Industrial Age had arrived.

There were many reasons England became the leader in the new technology. It had an abundance of the coal, iron, and water needed to power the new factories and machines. An extensive canal system, begun in 1761, transported fuel, raw materials, and finished goods across the country. The development of more productive agriculture and healthier livestock meant that a large portion of the workforce was free to shift from farming to manufacturing. The eradication of the plague had resulted in a healthier and longer-lived population, so there were not only more workers to produce goods but also more consumers to buy them. The money needed to build and run the factories came from the growing middle class. Thrifty, hard-working, and determined to succeed, English entrepreneurs who had earned money in overseas trade were willing to risk it in manufacturing, in order to create more wealth.

Lastly, unlike the rest of Europe or the Americas, England enjoyed peace at home from 1688 on. Although it sent soldiers to fight wars on both sides of the Atlantic, Britain itself remained safe. Peace gave it a big head start.

The changes brought by industrialization were rapid and drastic. In 1801, most people still lived on farms or in villages. By 1851, more than half lived in cities. Workers were crowded into miserable factory towns, where they inhabited foul slums without light or plumbing. Sanitation was so bad that sewage ran down the streets, and people died by the thousands from cholera, tuberculosis, and despair. These places were a lot like the fictional Coketown in Charles Dickens's novel *Hard Times:*

> *It was a town of machinery and tall chimneys, out of which interminable serpents of smoke trailed themselves for ever and ever, and never got uncoiled. It had a black canal in it, and a river that ran purple with ill-smelling dye, and vast piles of buildings full of windows where there was a rattling and a trembling all day long, and where the piston of the steam-engine worked monotonously up and down like the head of an elephant in a state of melancholy madness.*

Machines ran around the clock, and workers were forced to keep up. A typical working day was fourteen hours long. Men, women, and children kept up this grueling schedule six days a week, year after year after year. The result was broken bodies, broken spirits, and broken lives. The manufacturers and economists of the early nineteenth century thought that such unregulated working conditions were right and natural. According to "laissez-faire" economics, only if business was left free of interference would it prosper. Laws governing wages or hours would restrict the workings of a free marketplace, which would be bad for the economy and therefore for the country.

William Bell Scott's Iron and Coal *(1861) celebrates the power of the Industrial Revolution. Near the ironworkers, in the foreground, are an anchor, the air pump of a ship engine, the shells and barrel of a huge gun, and a drawing of a locomotive. Behind the workers can be seen a busy dock, a train steaming across a bridge, telegraph wires, and a smoking factory chimney.*

The most marvelous agent of change in these tumultuous times was the railway. In 1829, George Stephenson's steam-powered *Rocket* engine went an astounding twenty-four miles per hour, and Britain fell under the spell of the black, belching iron horse. The railway boom of the 1840s changed the face of England forever. "What a difference between now and then," says a character in one of English author William Thackeray's novels, recalling the time before railways. "Then was the old world. . . . But your railroad starts a new era. . . . We who lived before railways and survive out of the ancient world, are like father and Noah out of the Ark."

By the middle of the nineteenth century, more than 5,000 miles of railway stretched across Great Britain. The locomotive transformed many aspects of daily life. People who had never traveled more than a few miles from their villages could go into the city for a day's shopping or visit friends halfway across the country. A newspaper published in London could be read 180 miles away in Leeds. Perishables such as milk and fresh fish could be more easily transported from the country to the city. Soon fish-and-chips became the favorite food of London's working class.

And the iron horse accelerated the pace of industrialization. More railways meant more coal was dug up to power the engines and more iron produced to make the rails. Markets expanded and the prices of goods fell sharply as transport became much cheaper. By the middle of the nineteenth century, Britain produced about two-thirds of the world's coal, more than

half its iron, and more than half its cotton cloth. It truly was the "workshop of the world."

The changes brought by the Industrial Revolution were so rapid that society had to struggle to keep up. But it wasn't long before some people realized that political and social reform was needed, and needed immediately.

The Age of Reform

The violence of the French Revolution passed Britain by, but its ideas did not. For the first time, large numbers of people dared to think that Britain should be more democratic. Ideas about social equality gained ground not only among radical thinkers but among

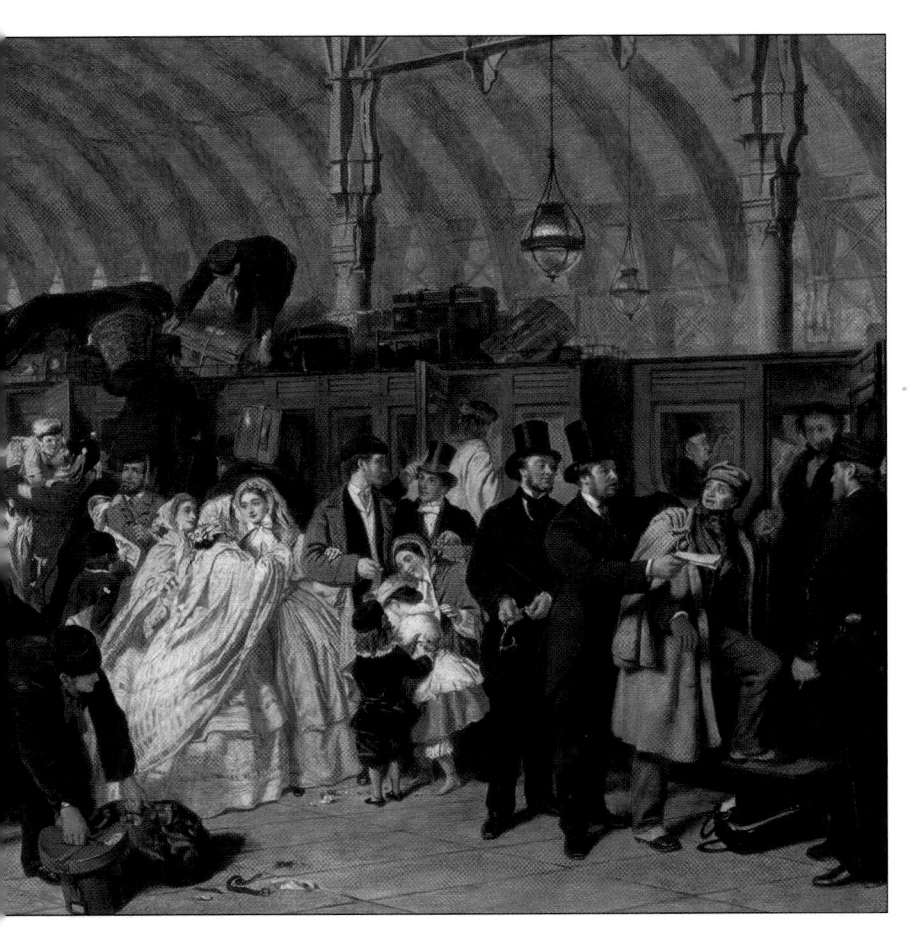

William Powell Frith's The Railway Station *(1863) presents a panorama of Victorian life. From left to right, you can see a working-class family heading for a third-class railway car, a middle-class family going on vacation, an upper-class wedding party, and a criminal being arrested by two detectives.* Everyone *in Victorian England traveled on the railways.*

laborers and members of the middle classes as well. The Industrial Revolution had created a whole new group of well-to-do manufacturers, financiers, and merchants who wanted more of a say in the way their country was governed.

At the beginning of the nineteenth century, only men of considerable property could vote. Of the 7 million adults living in England and Wales in 1830, only 435,000 landowners had the right to elect the members of Parliament. And because aristocratic landowners often handpicked their representatives, "rotten boroughs" with few inhabitants had more representatives than towns with large populations but few voters. New industrial cities such as Manchester and Birmingham had no MPs (members of Parliament), for instance, while small ancient villages might have two or three.

The demand for electoral reform gained ground in the early 1830s. Laborers, middle-class businessmen, and farmers alike pressed for reform. Conservatives (Tories) feared that enlarging the vote would ruin England. But Liberals (Whigs) pushed through reform, and in 1832 the First Reform Act became law. "The barriers of the constitution are broken down," the Conservative Duke of Wellington thundered. "The waters of destruction have burst the gates of the temple."

England, of course, was not destroyed. Moreover, the law did not deliver full democracy after all. Although the electorate was doubled, four out of five men still could not vote. But the bill did force the upper classes to share power with the middle classes—and it did so peacefully.

The Reform Act didn't affect working-class Britons at all. In fact, their situation grew worse. During the "Hungry Forties," harvests were bad, food prices were high, and people starved. Unhappy workers in search of a solution founded their own reform movement, called Chartism. The People's Charter demanded improvements such as universal male suffrage (voting rights), abolition of the requirement that members of Parliament be property owners, and the secret ballot. These demands were way ahead of their time. Although the Charter, with millions of signatures, was presented to Parliament three times, it was always rejected. Chartism eventually withered away. It would take two more Reform Acts, in 1867 and 1884, to give the total male working population the vote. Women were expressly excluded from the 1832 reforms. They had to wait for the vote until 1918.

Destitute families wait outside a poorhouse in Luke Fildes's Applicants for Admission to a Casual Ward *(1874).*

In 1848, Europe was swept by another round of revolutions. But England remained relatively calm. In part, perhaps, this was because of the traditional English respect for authority. But it was also because, even for the working classes, things were slowly getting better. As decade followed decade, peaceful reform occurred, one law at a time.

Reforms were fueled by moral outrage and an earnest desire to do good. Reformers were often crusading Protestants called Evangelicals, who made it their business to educate the public about contemporary evils. For instance, slavery was abolished throughout the British Empire in 1834 after an Evangelical MP named William Wilberforce flooded the country with antislavery pamphlets. (Slavery in Britain itself had been explicitly outlawed since 1772.)

Reformers also turned their attention to the conditions of lower-class life. A series of official reports called Blue Books revealed to a shocked public many of the abuses of the industrial system. Britons learned that in the mines, women and children as young as five worked on their hands and knees, pushing loaded

Filthy slums such as this, common in every major Victorian city, were breeding grounds for crime, disease, and despair.

cars up mine shafts. In textile mills, children worked sixteen-hour days in rooms heated as high as eighty-five degrees. In some slums, as many as two or three families occupied a single room, often six or seven to a bed, attempting to survive without ventilation, light, or sanitation.

All these revelations produced a steady stream of reforms, often passed over the protests of factory owners and landlords. For instance, the Factory Act of 1833 decreed that no child under nine could work in the cotton mills, and those between nine and thirteen could work only eight hours a day. The Ten Hours Act of 1847 limited the hours both women and children could work in the mines. The Public Health Act of 1848 took measures to regulate building and sanitation codes. And so on. Slowly conditions improved for even the poorest of workers.

Reforms affected the whole of Victorian society. By stages, the death penalty was restricted, imprisonment for debt was eliminated, and public hanging was abolished. Prisons were made more sanitary and humane, and public education became more widely available. The "sports" of bull- and bearbaiting were outlawed. The police force was expanded and became more efficient. Altogether, Victorian life became more civilized and more humane.

By the middle of the nineteenth century, Britain was the richest country in the world. It led in shipping, banking, and manufacturing. The value of British exports doubled between the years 1842 and 1870. The large middle class was more comfortable than ever before. And so were the working classes, whose members were able to afford some of the items—ready-made clothes, canned goods—so temptingly offered by the new industries.

The Victorians celebrated their prosperity with the Crystal Palace Exhibition of 1851. The exhibition showed them at their best—inventive, generous, proud of their accomplishments, and eager to celebrate those of others. The Crystal Palace was the climax of Queen Victoria's reign and of her personal life as well. Mid-Victorian prosperity would last for twenty-five years and would make many citizens quite content.

The British Empire

Great Britain had emerged from the Napoleonic Wars in 1815 as the strongest power in Europe, possibly in the world. But England was not interested in military conquest in Europe itself. Instead, it intended to use its naval superiority to protect itself against foreign involvement and guard its trading routes. For most of the century, Britain pursued a policy of "splendid isolation." It didn't want anything to do with Europe's messy wars and revolutions.

Only once did Britain let down its guard. That was in 1854, when it sided with France and Turkey against Russia in the Crimean War. (Russia was seeking to control the Dardanelles—the narrow strait between Europe and Turkey—and thus posed a threat to England's Mediterranean sea routes.) Almost immediately, the government discovered it had made a mistake. British military leaders were incompetent, the supply system was inefficient, and disease among the troops was rampant. In short, the war was a disaster. Its most famous moment was the doomed charge of 673

THE CRYSTAL PALACE

On May 1, 1851, the first world's fair opened in Hyde Park, London. Officially called the Great Exhibition of the Works of Industry of All Nations, it was better known as the Crystal Palace. The exhibition hall itself was a truly spectacular sight. A revolutionary building made of iron and 293,655 panes of glass, it covered seventeen acres and was tall enough to enclose the giant elms of the park. The architect, Joseph Paxton, assembled it from factory-made parts in just six months.

The exhibition was the inspiration of Prince Albert, who wanted a showcase for the technological achievements of not just Britain but the world. On opening day, Queen Victoria was bursting with pride: "The tremendous cheering, the joy expressed on every face, the vastness of the building . . . and my beloved husband, the creator of this peace festival uniting industry and art of all nations of the earth. . . . God bless my dearest Albert, and my dear country, which has shown itself so great today."

The queen returned to the Crystal Palace forty times—and no wonder. The wealth and variety of exhibits seemed never-ending. There were 109,000 items on display—silks and carpets from Turkey, watches from Switzerland, the Jacquard loom from France, the McCormick reaper and bowie knives from America, steelmaking displays and steam engines from Britain, an envelope machine, ladies' corsets, celluloid (plastic) collars, and the first yellow pencil. Fittingly, more than half of the exhibits were British.

A financial and public relations triumph, the Crystal Palace drew 6,200,000 visitors in six months. "This is England," the exhibition proclaimed to an admiring world. "Look what we can do."

The queen and Prince Albert open the Crystal Palace Exhibition on May 1, 1851. Towering above them is one of the great elms of Hyde Park.

British cavalrymen down into a valley defended by Russian guns, immortalized by Alfred, Lord Tennyson in "The Charge of the Light Brigade":

Cannon to the right of them
Cannon to the left of them,
Cannon in front of them
Volleyed and thundered
Stormed at with shot and shell,
Boldly they rode and well,
Into the jaws of Death
Into the mouth of Hell
Rode the six hundred.

As a contemporary said, the Crimean War was a crime. At least it was a well-documented crime, for it was the first modern war to be covered by a journalist at the front. A London *Times* reporter sent back such horrific reports that the government was forced to send an intrepid young nurse named Florence Nightingale out to the Crimea with supplies, medicine, and trained assistants. She reduced the death toll in the military hospital at Scutari from 40 percent to 2 percent, and founded modern nursing in the process.

England did not fight in another European war until World War I began in 1914. But it was deeply involved with nations around the world as trading partners and colonies. By the mid-nineteenth century, Britain's empire stretched around the globe, and it kept growing. It expanded by fits and starts, with no overall plan. In order to control overseas markets, Britain often took over the administration of a foreign country, as in India or Egypt. British troops might find themselves defending local rulers who cooperated with British authority, or putting down native rebellions. Sometimes imperialist expansion was motivated by national security, as in Ireland, and sometimes by the need to get rid of an unwanted population, as in Australia. It could even be motivated by humanitarian ideals, as when antislavery crusaders urged Britain to take over the Sudan in order to abolish slavery there.

The consequences of British imperialism would be many and profound, both for Britain and the world. The British Empire began with

Florence Nightingale (center) *and her nurses care for soldiers in the British hospital at Scutari during the Crimean War. After the war, Nightingale became the first woman to be awarded the British Order of Merit.*

Ireland, and in the nineteenth century Ireland continued to present more problems than any other British colony.

Ireland

England had ruled Ireland since the twelfth century, when an English king landed there and began to grant Irish land to his nobles. In the 1500s, the Protestant Reformation turned Britain officially Protestant and King Henry VIII established a national church, the Church of England, or Anglican Church. Ireland, however, remained Catholic. Irish Catholics hated to have to pay tithes, or taxes, to the Anglican Church. They also resented being dependent on England for imported coal.

For the next 150 years, Catholics were systematically thrown off ancestral land and replaced by Protestants loyal to the English throne. The pattern of oppression continued with the passage of the Penal Laws in the 1690s. These laws forbade Catholics to purchase or inherit land, vote, hold public office, own a gun, become teachers or lawyers, or attend Catholic schools.

The Act of Union that created the United Kingdom in 1801 abolished the Irish Parliament but allowed the Irish people to vote for representatives in the British Parliament. However, they had to vote for Protestants, since no Catholic could be an MP. This was overturned by the Catholic Emancipation Act of 1829, which allowed Catholics to hold public office. But after centuries of unjust treatment, many Irish still hated the union with Great Britain.

Then disaster struck. In 1845, a fungus destroyed the potato crop, the staple food of Ireland. The stinking black rot spread from the leaves down to the tubers, laying waste to fields and sickening people. The Great Potato Famine lasted five years. Over a period of ten years, approximately a million and a half people died and some two million emigrated to Britain and the United States. The English government didn't do much to help. Laissez-faire economists held fast to the principle that it was better to let people starve than to interfere with the "natural" laws of supply and demand. The British could have saved lives by importing food in bulk to Ireland, but they imported very little, and it came too late. The Irish never forgave them.

A British family emigrates to a distant land in Ford Madox Brown's painting The Last of England *(1855). (Note the tiny hand peeking out from beneath the woman's cloak.) Between 1845 and 1900, more than ten million people left the British Isles in search of a better life. Most went to the United States, while others traveled to Canada or Australia.*

So Ireland remained poverty-stricken, and in the late 1850s, an Irish liberation group called the Fenians began to call for complete separation from Britain. Prime Minister William Gladstone swore that he would calm down the situation and "pacify Ireland." He passed Irish land reform measures and finally began to press for Home Rule (a separate Irish Parliament). But no version of Irish self-government ever passed both houses of Parliament during Victoria's reign, and the problem persisted into the twentieth century, when it would cause more bloodshed and terror.

Australia

Britain first claimed Australia in 1770, when Captain James Cook landed on the continent's fertile eastern shore. The first settlement in Australia was a penal colony for British convicts, set up in Botany Bay in 1788. Soon other settlers found their way to Australia. Throughout the nineteenth century, the population of the British Isles grew faster than the job market. So the government began to encourage emigration to the colonies. In the first half of the century, thousands took the long sea voyage from England, Scotland, and Ireland to raise sheep in the Australian interior. A gold rush in 1851 brought another flood of settlers. By the end of the century, Australia was wealthy.

India

The British first came to India in 1600, when the British East India Company established trading posts along the coast. Gradually, the company expanded its holdings, until by the Victorian Age it ruled much of the Indian subcontinent. Its authority ended abruptly in 1857, with the Indian Mutiny (Indians call it the First War for Independence).

The immediate cause of the mutiny was the cartridge for a new rifle. The cartridge had to be bitten before it was loaded into the gun. Rumors spread among Muslim soldiers in the British Indian army that the cartridge was greased with pig fat (which violated Muslim law against eating pork), and among Hindu soldiers that it was greased with cow fat (which violated Hindu law, which held the cow sacred). They were both right. Outraged Indian soldiers (sepoys) rose up against their officers and murdered most of the Europeans living in Delhi. The British retaliated with savage force. After the mutiny was put down the next year, the British Crown took over the administration of India from the East India Company.

The Raj, as British rule of India was known (from the Hindu word for "king"), was the "jewel in the crown" of the British Empire. About one-third of India was governed by Indian rulers under the advice of the British. The rest was run by the British-dominated Indian Civil Service. The British themselves held all the important posts in the service and established a miniature British society many miles from home. Anglo-Indians enjoyed English polo clubs, country clubs, tea dances, garden parties, and balls. By the 1890s, the two hundred thousand Britons in India governed about one-fifth of the human race. It was the largest overseas empire any country has ever owned.

Africa

From the 1840s on, British explorers and missionaries ventured into the interior of Africa to seek adventure and convert the inhabitants to Christianity. A race to discover the source of the Nile was won by John Speke in 1858, when he traced the river to Lake Victoria. Official involvement with the African continent intensified with the completion of the Suez Canal in Egypt in 1869. The canal shortened the route to India and the Far East (ships used to have to go all the way around the Cape of Good Hope, at the continent's southern tip). It also meant that, in order to protect trade links, Britain had to become involved in the politics and conflicts of northern Africa.

Imperialist Europe realized that Africa was available for the taking. At the Berlin Conference in 1884, fourteen nations, including Belgium, France, Germany, Great Britain, Spain, Portugal, Turkey, and the United States, got together to divide up Africa among them. The subsequent free-for-all was called the Scramble for Africa. Most of Africa would remain in European possession until after World War II, some seventy years later.

African adventures made two Victorian heroes very famous. General Charles Gordon was a model Victorian soldier—courageous, resolute, incorruptible. He died in 1885 in the siege of Khartoum, defending Egyptian Sudan against the forces of a fanatical rebel called the Mahdi. Britain held its breath as a relief force inched its way toward the besieged city—and reached it two days late. The city had already been taken and the defenders killed. Gordon became an instant martyr.

The other hero, Dr. David Livingstone, was an explorer and a missionary who wanted to spread Christianity and abolish slavery throughout Africa. (Long after the British had abolished it in the colonies, the slave trade persisted within Africa itself.) By opening trade routes throughout the continent, he hoped to bring prosperity to central Africa and undercut the trade in human beings. Livingstone penetrated ever deeper into the interior, becoming the first European to see Victoria Falls and the Zambezi River. In about 1870, he lost contact with the world. By then, he was so renowned that a New York newspaper sent a journalist named Henry Stanley to eastern Africa to find him. On the shore of Lake Tanganyika, Stanley saw a white man coming toward him.

"Dr. Livingstone, I presume?" Stanley asked.

Although ill, Livingstone refused to leave Africa. When he died two years later, his body was sent to England, where he was buried in Westminster Abbey.

South Africa

England first established a foothold in South Africa in 1815, when it founded a trading post on the Cape of Good Hope. Although white farmers of Dutch descent, known as the Boers, already held most of the land in the region, British traders and settlers continued to arrive. To rid themselves of the British, the independent Boers made the Great Trek northward between 1835 and 1843. Settling in northern South Africa, the Boers established the republics of Orange Free State and Transvaal, independent of the British Cape Colony. When deposits of diamonds and gold were discovered in the Transvaal in the 1870s and 1880s, British foreigners (Uitlanders) streamed in. Cecil Rhodes, prime minister of the Cape Colony, was determined to annex the Boer republics.

The Boer War began in 1899 with a string of Boer victories. The British were shocked that their well-trained troops were losing to a bunch of farmers. Old and ailing, Queen Victoria rallied the country. "We are not interested in the possibilities of defeat," she announced. "They do not exist." The British brought in reinforcements from Canada, Australia, and New Zealand, and finally the Boers were subdued—officially. But Boer commando units continued to fight a guerrilla war, and atrocities were committed. In desperation, the British removed whole farming families to concentration camps, where some twenty thousand Boer women and children died. In 1902, the Boer states became part of the British Cape Colony.

During the 217-day siege of the British garrison at Mafeking at the start of the war, Colonel Robert Baden-Powell organized the boys of

Boer soldiers attack a British convoy on February 25, 1902.

the town and turned them into scouts and spies. Back in England several years later, he founded the Boy Scout movement to give city boys outdoor training.

End of a Century

The golden glow of Victorian prosperity and the Crystal Palace Exhibition lasted until the 1870s. Then, gradually, the national mood darkened. Victoria still ruled the nation, the British navy ruled the seas, and the British pound ruled the world, but the British people themselves were not quite as optimistic and confident as they had been at midcentury. All the reforms of the century had not brought the equality of opportunity and general well-being that many had hoped for, and they wondered why. Radical movements sprang up—women's rights, Irish Home Rule, trade unionism, expansion of the franchise. Gradually, more groups of people became politically active.

Two giants dominated British politics in the last half of the century: Benjamin Disraeli and William Gladstone. Disraeli (1804–1881), witty, learned, cynical, and charming, was a British Jew who had been baptized into the Christian faith when he was a boy. A Conservative, he supported landowners, the Anglican Church, and British imperialism. "Dizzie" was a great friend of Queen Victoria, who adored him. ("Everyone likes flattery," he once told a friend, "and when it comes to royalty you should lay it on with a trowel.") He was the one who proclaimed the queen empress of India—a mostly symbolic title for which she rewarded him with an earldom.

Gladstone (1809–1898), moral, earnest, and a Liberal, could not have been more different. Unlike his imperialist opponent, he favored Irish Home Rule and self-government for the colonies. Queen Victoria, who never liked Gladstone's cold and formal manner, once complained that he "speaks to me as if I was a public meeting."

Despite their political differences, both the Conservative and Liberal parties passed a number of important reform bills in these years, including laws regulating food purity, improving housing and sanitation, and legalizing unions. Some of the most important of these laws, the 1870 and 1880 Education Acts, established state-supported schools and ordered compulsory (required by law) education for children up to age eleven. By the time the Third Reform Act was passed in 1884, giving the vote to most working-class men, there were ten times as many voters as there had been in 1830. Real political power had passed from the hands of the large landowners to the middle classes. Britain was becoming truly democratic.

Above all, the last two decades of the Victorian Age saw the triumph of imperialism. Britain was in a frenzy of colonial acquisition: Burma (now Myanmar) and Malaysia, Kenya and Tanzania, Fiji and the Falkland Islands. By 1900, more than seventy colonies and occupied territories—one-quarter of the globe—were under British rule. As their flag was raised across the globe, the English people could say with pride, "The sun never sets on the British Empire."

The Queen's Diamond Jubilee of 1897, commemorating sixty years of rule, showcased her empire. Soldiers from all over the world marched in a military procession past her reviewing stand: Maoris from New Zealand, Mounties from Canada, Gurkhas from India, troops from the West Indies, Sierra Leone, Cyprus, and Borneo. The climax of the show, a spectacular naval review, boasted 173 ships, the pride of the royal fleet. On the night of the jubilee, Queen Victoria tapped out a telegraph message

Queen Victoria receives the tribute of her people on her Diamond Jubilee, June 22, 1897. Afterward, the queen wrote in her diary, "No one, ever, I believe, has met with such an ovation as was given to me. . . . The crowds were quite indescribable, and their enthusiasm truly marvelous and deeply touching."

for her subjects that was seen instantly around the world: "From my heart I thank my beloved people. May God bless them."

It was the last hurrah of the Victorian Age. The queen died just four years later, in January 1901. Crowds thronged the streets of London, which were decorated as she had instructed, in white and purple. An editorial in a popular newspaper read:

> *The Queen is dead. No language can express the sense of personal loss. . . . Few of us, perhaps, have realized till now how large a part she had in the life of every-one of us; how the thread of her life . . . has touched and brightened the life of each and all her subjects.*

Those watching the funeral procession were Victorians no longer. The twentieth century had officially begun.

CHAPTER TWO

A Popular Art

To the ever-busy Victorians, art was yet another outlet for their boundless energy. They poured that energy into creation—the longest novels, the most detailed paintings, the biggest and most elaborate buildings. The result of all this frenetic activity was masterpieces that we still enjoy today.

Romanticism and Realism

The Victorians were heirs to the eighteenth-century Romantic movement in literature and art, which stressed the power of the imagination and the importance of individual experience. Rejecting the ordered serenity of classical (ancient Greek and Roman) art, Romantic artists were drawn to the mystical architecture and rich pageantry of the Middle Ages, to untamed nature, and to the supernatural. The nature poetry of William Wordsworth, the medieval history novels of Sir Walter Scott, and the mystical drawings of William Blake all exemplified the spirit of Romanticism.

Early Victorians were also Romantics. But as the age went on, their Romanticism came to be more and more tempered by realism. Charles Dickens's novels, for instance, are dramatic, even melodramatic stories of adventure, mystery, and ideal love, but they are also detailed studies of everyday life. Robert Browning's poems are set in the far-off worlds of Renaissance Italy or medieval England, but they are also precise and candid portraits of very individual characters, warts and all. By the end of the century, realism in art had become social realism, concerned with the grittier aspects of modern life, as in the novels of Thomas Hardy or the street scenes of Luke Fildes.

The tension between realism and Romanticism lasted throughout the Victorian Age and gave to its art both an emotional intensity and an endless fascination with detail.

In The Hay Wain *(1821), John Constable captures the beauty of the English countryside.*

The Reading Public

Victorians loved to read. They were hungry for information, eager for inspiration, happy to be entertained. With none of the visual media we rely on today for amusement—no TV, movies, videos, or computers—they depended on the written word to put them in touch with the wider world. The result was a huge outpouring of imaginative and nonfiction writing, in novels, poetry, journals, newspapers, and pamphlets.

Not all Victorians were voracious readers. At the beginning

A man reads the newspaper aloud to his family in a country cottage. During the nineteenth century, more people of all classes learned to read.

of the period, few members of the working class had either the leisure or the ability to read. Many people who could *officially* read—that is, sign their names in the church register—could barely get through a line of text. But the literacy rate climbed steadily throughout the century, rising from 67 percent of males and 51 percent of females in 1841 to about 97 percent overall in 1900.

Better education, increased wealth, and the growth of the middle class all contributed to an unprecedented audience for the printed word. So did improved technology. The steam-driven printing press made printed materials cheaper and more available than ever before, resulting in the first age of mass communication. And the printing press made the best-selling Victorian novel possible.

The Novel

On a fall day in 1841, anxious crowds waited on the docks in New York City. "Is Little Nell dead?" they shouted to an incoming ship. They weren't asking about a real person. They were worried about a character in a novel. They were waiting for the latest installment in Charles Dickens's novel *The Old Curiosity Shop*. Eight-year-old Little Nell was very sick. Had she died?

She had, and the world mourned. A British member of Parliament read the death scene on a train. "He should not have killed her!" he exclaimed, and threw the book out the window.

Today readers often find Little Nell's death too sentimental. But the death of children was all too common in the nineteenth century, and men, women, and children could deeply sympathize with the fate of a fictitious little girl. The universality of the public's sorrow also demonstrated the extraordinary popularity of fiction in the nineteenth century. Everybody, it seemed, was reading the same book at the same time.

The English novel had been born more than a century earlier, with the adventures of a shipwrecked sailor named Robinson Crusoe on a desert island. By the nineteenth century, the novel had matured into a complicated narrative about the relationships of men and women in society. Usually nineteenth-century novels trace the progress of a protagonist through the entanglements of family life, work, and romance. They star some of the most memorable heroes in literature—Oliver Twist, David Copperfield, Jane Eyre, Heathcliff, Becky Sharp, Adam Bede, Jude Fawley. Four hundred to one thousand pages each, Victorian novels are so long and complicated that a later writer called them "loose baggy monsters." Partly this was because many novels were first published chapter by chapter in literary journals. The more chapters, the more money an author made.

Novels were also long because novelists were attempting to capture a whole world. A panorama of the Victorian Age comes crowding onto their pages—upper-class drawing rooms and poverty-stricken hovels, grimy industrial cities and rustic villages, American swamps, Parisian prisons, and the Swiss Alps. Although they are long, they are anything but dull. Novelists prided themselves on hair-raising plots that had readers turning the pages. Do you want to read about an orphan boy who is arrested for theft, saved from prison by a kindhearted gentleman, kidnapped by thieves, and finally rescued by a woman who is later murdered? How about a pair of lovers doomed in a volcanic eruption, or a man who loses his life on the guillotine, or a boy who finds a buried treasure? Try a Victorian novel—namely *Oliver Twist, The Last Days of Pompeii, A Tale of Two Cities*, or *Treasure Island.*

Here are some other wonderful reads:

David Copperfield by Charles Dickens (1850)

This very long novel (around nine hundred pages) about an orphan boy who grows up to be a writer is based in part on the author's own life. From David's early job in a shoe-blacking factory to his experiences at school and his first infatuation with the delicious but dim-witted Dora Spenlow, Dickens drew on his own youthful emotions and experiences. The novel contains some of Dickens's most memorable characters: the luckless but hopeful Mr. Micawber, the half-mad Mr. Dick, the tyrannical stepfather Mr. Murdstone, and the oily blackmailer Uriah Heep. At the end of the journey, when all the plot threads are tied up and dozens of characters are married off, buried, sent abroad, or otherwise disposed of, readers feel that they've had a fascinating glimpse into Victorian life.

Jane Eyre by Charlotte Brontë (1847)

A penniless girl becomes a governess, falls in love with her mysterious employer, is driven away by his dark secret, and eventually unites with her truelove (we're not telling who). Sound familiar? That's because *Jane Eyre* is the first, and best, gothic romance. Like *David Copperfield,* it begins when its main character is still a child, and it lets the reader watch a scared girl grow up into a self-assured young woman. And in the end? As Jane tells us, "Reader, I married him."

Dr. Jekyll and Mr. Hyde by Robert Louis Stevenson (1886)

Not a novel but a long short story, *The Strange Case of Dr. Jekyll and Mr. Hyde* is a horror classic. The kindly Dr. Jekyll, fascinated by the evil that

We might imagine that this Victorian young lady is reading David Copperfield*—were it not for the slimness of the volume she holds! England is famous for the great novels it produced in the nineteenth century.*

lurks in all good men, concocts a potion to bring out his own dark side. The bestial Mr. Hyde embarks on an independent, murderous career that Jekyll cannot control. In the end, Jekyll must commit suicide to kill off his demonic second self.

THE INIMITABLE BOZ

Most people would agree that Charles Dickens (1812–1870) was one of the greatest English novelists of all time. The "Inimitable Boz" was born to a lower-middle-class family in the seaside town of Portsmouth. His father, a charming spendthrift, spent his way into debtor's prison, and twelve-year-old Charles was forced to go to work at a shoe-blacking factory, where he labeled bottles for twelve hours a day. The experience of being abandoned and alone marked him for life. It also gave him a profound sympathy with the poor and the oppressed, especially children.

His father eventually managed to pay off his debts and Charles went back to school. He taught himself shorthand and by age sixteen was working as a parliamentary and court reporter. With much nervousness, he submitted his first literary sketch of London life to a magazine—and saw it printed with his pen name, Boz. The collected *Sketches by Boz* (1836) was so popular that he was asked to write his first novel, *Pickwick Papers* (1837).

Pickwick was an amazing, unheard-of triumph. The country was swept by a wave of Pickwick enthusiasm. There were Pickwick coats, Pickwick canes, and Pickwick cigars; there were literary rip-offs and unauthorized stage adaptations. A British tourist was reported to have carved "Pickwick" on one of the Egyptian pyramids. Dickens suddenly found himself world famous. He was twenty-four years old.

Success enabled the young author to marry. He eventually had ten children to support—as well as his always needy parents and brothers and sisters. For the rest of his life, Dickens drove himself to produce. He wrote fifteen novels in all (one unfinished), in addition to four travel books and countless stories and articles. Ever since, his writings have re-created Victorian England for his readers.

Dickens's flamboyant, exaggerated style has led some critics to call him overly sentimental and melodramatic. But he wasn't afraid to tackle hard social problems—industrialization in *Hard Times,* abusive schools in *Nicholas Nickleby,* street poverty in *Bleak House,* poorhouses in *Oliver Twist.* The dynamic energy of his novels mirrors that of his era. He walked for hours through the streets of London, visiting its hospitals, prisons, poorhouses, markets, operas, theaters, and concert

rooms, trying to see and experience everything for himself.

Although he dealt with some serious subjects, Dickens wasn't a grim or tragic writer. His novels end happily, for Dickens had a comic vision. The age in which he lived was basically optimistic, and so was he.

In the later years of his life, Dickens gave a series of dramatic readings of his works, which were wildly popular. But they wore him out, and he died relatively young, at age fifty-eight. One scholar said that Dickens "made out of Victorian England a complete world, with a life and vigor and idiom [language] of its own, quite unlike any other world there has ever been." In English literature, only Shakespeare created such a brilliant imaginary world and is so beloved by so many people.

A scared-looking Oliver is introduced to Fagin and his den of thieves in one of George Cruikshank's illustrations for Charles Dickens's Oliver Twist. *The thrilling story of the orphan Oliver was an immediate success when it was published in 1838.*

Robert Louis Stevenson was also one of the century's greatest writers for children. The Victorian era was the beginning of a golden age of children's books, which continued into the next century. There were animal stories such as Anna Sewell's *Black Beauty,* tales of adventure such as Stevenson's *Treasure Island* and *Kidnapped,* and fantasies including George MacDonald's *The Princess and the Goblins.* Most famous are Lewis Carroll's nonsense classics *Alice's Adventures in Wonderland* and *Through the Looking Glass,* about a little girl who falls down a rabbit hole into an upside-down world of talking caterpillars and quarrelsome playing cards.

The Mad Hatter, the Dormouse, and the March Hare join Alice at an unusual tea party in Sir John Tenniel's illustration for Lewis Carroll's Alice's Adventures in Wonderland.

Poetry and Drama

The Victorians also had a great appetite for poetry. Schoolchildren recited poetry on graduation day, and families read their favorite poets around the hearth on a winter's eve. The age's most popular poet was Alfred, Lord Tennyson, named England's poet laureate in 1850. He fulfilled his official role by writing decent "occasional poetry" celebrating the Crystal Palace or the queen. Many of his best poems are dramatic monologues, or soliloquies, that bring to life some aspect of the speaker's character. "Ulysses," for instance, is told by the wandering hero of ancient Greek myths, now an old man and about to set off on life's last voyage.

Another Victorian poet, Robert Browning, is also known for his dramatic monologues. In these conversational poems, characters expose their true selves. A dying Renaissance bishop reveals his preference for material things over God, a duke unintentionally admits that he murdered his last wife, a monk discloses his love of art. Browning's poems are vivid and crackling with energy.

Much Victorian poetry consists of lyric, or songlike, short verses that express a mood. It is often about nature, or death, or love, like the first stanza of "A Birthday" (1857) by Christina Rossetti:

My heart is like a singing bird
Whose nest is in a watered shoot:
My heart is like an apple tree
Whose boughs are bent with thickset fruit;
My heart is like a rainbow shell
That paddles in a halcyon sea;
My heart is gladder than all these
Because my love is come to me.

Not all Victorian poetry is serious. It can be lighthearted and whimsical, like the nonsense verses of Lewis Carroll and Edward Lear. Lear is famous for his limericks:

There is a young lady, whose nose
Continually prospers and grows;
When it grew out of sight,
She exclaimed in a fright,
"Oh! Farewell to the end of my nose!"

Theater and Music

Victorians poured all their dramatic genius into their novels and poetry. Their drama was, for the most part, not very good. Plays in the nineteenth century, although popular and well attended, were usually melodramatic or stiff and moralistic. Not until the very end of the century did two really talented playwrights emerge: Oscar Wilde and George Bernard Shaw. Wilde wore velvet knee breeches and a green carnation in his buttonhole in defiance of the sober, respectable male dress of the day. He was known for his brilliant conversation and clever sayings. "A little sincerity is a dangerous thing," he once said, "and a great deal of it is absolutely fatal." His plays poked fun at Victorian propriety and self-importance. His masterpiece was *The Importance of Being Earnest,* first presented in 1895.

In the 1890s, Anglo-Irish playwright George Bernard Shaw presented the first of more than thirty full-length plays. He wrote plays such as *Arms and the Man* (1894) and *Major Barbara* (1905) not only to reform society, but also to make people laugh. Shaw delighted audiences with his wit and sense of fun.

The end of the century also saw the emergence of another enormously popular dramatic form, the comic operetta. Witty and hummable works by W. S. Gilbert and Arthur Sullivan, including *The Pirates of Penzance* (1880) and *The Mikado* (1885), amused audiences with their clever lyrics and up-to-date references.

Victorians also loved going to music halls and listening to band concerts in the park. Although they were admirers of contemporary European music—Victoria and Albert were friends of German composer Felix Mendelssohn, for instance—the British created no great classical music of their own. The greatest musicians of the nineteenth century—Beethoven, Schubert, Mendelssohn, Tchaikovsky, Wagner, Verdi, Mahler, and others—all came from the European continent.

Art and Architecture

In the nineteenth century, art was more important in the cultural life of England than it had ever been before—or has been since. Increased wealth meant more picture buying, and great numbers of people went to picture galleries, especially the yearly Royal Academy Exhibitions. Middle-class families hung hand-colored prints of famous paintings on

A poster advertises Gilbert and Sullivan's D'Oyly Carte Opera Company. The pair's fast-paced, funny operettas were often set in exotic locales, such as Venice, Italy (The Gondoliers), *or Japan* (The Mikado).

their walls. Prints made from a sentimental portrait of a young girl, *Cherry Ripe* (1879) by the most popular Victorian painter, John Everett Millais, sold 600,000 copies—and another 400,000 customers wanted it.

In the first half of the century, Romantic landscape painting was at its peak. Working from hundreds of open-air sketches, John Constable rendered the beauty of Britain's meadows, mountains, brooks, and streams. In his landscapes, he tried to capture the ever-changing drama of "light and shadow that never stand still." His contemporary, Joseph Mallord William Turner, has been called the greatest British painter of all time. His paintings explore the conflict between humankind and the forces of nature, with people overwhelmed by storm, avalanche, mountains, and the sea. Constable described Turner's work as "airy visions, painted with tinted steam," because his painting became more impressionistic as the artist got older. Many critics think it looked forward to the abstract painting of the twentieth century.

THE PRE-RAPHAELITES

In 1850, a brilliantly colored picture called *Christ in the House of His Parents* was displayed at the annual Royal Academy Exhibition. It was unusual because, although it had a religious theme, the young Jesus, his mother, and his father were not idealized. They looked like ordinary people from the English countryside. Critics called it "revolting," "disgusting," and "hideous."

The painter, John Everett Millais, was a member of the Pre-Raphaelite Brotherhood, a group of young painters and poets who wanted to revolutionize art. They called themselves Pre-Raphaelites because, they said, they wanted to return to the purity of form and "truth to nature" of Italian Renaissance art before Raphael. Actually they knew little about Renaissance art, and their own paintings looked decidedly un-Italian. But Millais and his colleague Holman Hunt did produce extraordinarily detailed, brilliantly colored scenes painted in the open air with live models. Their idea of "truth to nature" was so literal that practically every leaf in their paintings can be counted.

Despite some initial resistance, their detailed realism, combined with their poetic subject matter—they favored themes from the Bible, Shakespeare, and medieval history—eventually made them popular. People were fascinated by their painstaking naturalism. To the Pre-Raphaelites, painting from life meant exactly that. Millais insisted that his model for the painting *Ophelia* (1852) lie for many hours in a bathtub filled with water. She caught a bad cold and almost died—all for the sake of art!

Another Pre-Raphaelite, Dante Gabriel Rossetti, produced mystical paintings of long-necked, longhaired women. Their brooding sensuousness created a new ideal of Victorian beauty.

The Pre-Raphaelites influenced many other Victorian artists. Millais went on to become the most successful artist of his day and was eventually elected president of the Royal Academy. The group's most lasting influence, though, was through a later member, a textile and furniture designer named William Morris. He founded the Arts and Crafts movement to revive handmade design techniques almost lost through industrialization. Morris's wallpaper and fabric designs are still used and admired by people today.

The beautiful women in Dante Gabriel Rossetti's paintings seem lost in an eternal daydream.

Turner was never popular with most of the British public. They wanted detailed, realistic paintings that told a story. One sentimental favorite, for instance, was *The Old Shepherd's Chief Mourner* (c. 1837) by Sir Edwin Landseer, which shows a melancholy dog resting its head on the coffin of its late master. Sometimes paintings could be "read," detail by detail, like a book. *The Last Day in the Old Home* (1862) by Robert Martineau portrays a family forced to sell its ancestral estate. Every detail, from the gambling slips lying on the floor, to the auctioneer removing objects for sale, to the husband raising a glass of champagne, reveals that the family has been ruined by the man's drinking and gaming. Victorians especially loved art that taught a moral lesson.

The panoramic paintings of William Powell Frith are practically whole novels in themselves. A painting such as *Derby Day*

A dog mourns for its departed master in Sir Edwin Landseer's The Old Shepherd's Chief Mourner *(c. 1837), one of the best-loved of all Victorian paintings. Every detail tells a story—the spectacles sitting on the Bible, the now useless tam-o'-shanter (woolen cap), the shepherd's crook lying on the floor.*

(c. 1856), with its gamblers, acrobats, beggars, fortune-tellers, flower girls, dogs, horses, and upper-class spectators, is a true social documentary. People at the Royal Academy Exhibition were so fascinated by its wealth of detail that guards had to erect rails to protect the painting from crowds of eager viewers.

By the end of the nineteenth century, many artists had rejected the idea that art had to convey a social message. Rather, they said, the aim of art was the pursuit of beauty—art for art's sake. American artist James McNeill Whistler, who settled in London at age twenty-five, scandalized the art world in 1875 with his almost abstract *Nocturne in Black and Gold: The Falling Rocket.* Art critic John Ruskin said the work was like "flinging a pot of paint in the public's face."

Victorian architecture was a mixture of nostalgia and modernity. The Romantic movement made neo-Gothicism, inspired by medieval architecture, the most popular contemporary style. The best example of neo-Gothicism was the new Houses of Parliament, begun in 1834 after the old Parliament buildings burned down. One of the century's most influential architects, A. W. Pugin, designed the richly decorated interior. Victorian architecture also used lots of new materials, particularly iron. Iron columns and arches supported the roofs of the immense new railroad stations. The iron and glass structure of the Crystal Palace was so far ahead of its time that nothing like it would be seen again until the skyscrapers of the twentieth century.

The Houses of Parliament, built in 1834, are the most famous example of neo-Gothic architecture in Great Britain.

CHAPTER THREE

Faith and Doubt

Victorians were dutiful, moral, and religious. They were also plagued by doubt, as the century's scientific discoveries conflicted with deeply held beliefs that were thousands of years old.

A National Church

On Sunday, March 30, 1851, a national survey discovered that 60 percent of the British population was in church. Of these, 47 percent were Anglican, 49 percent were Nonconformist, and 4 percent were Catholic. At the midpoint of the Victorian Age, Great Britain was a churchgoing nation.

The British Isles had been Christian since the sixth century, when the pope sent Saint Augustine to convert the Anglo-Saxons. A thousand years later, during the Protestant Reformation, King Henry VIII broke with the Roman Catholic Church and established the Church of England, or Anglican Church, with himself at the head. In Victorian England, the Anglican was still the official church, and the country was still overwhelmingly Protestant.

All Protestants were not Anglicans, however. Even after it had separated from Rome, the Church of England kept a hierarchy of bishops and archbishops and retained a set order of prayers for weekly services. Other Protestants, such as Presbyterians, Methodists, Congregationalists, and Quakers, had a much less elaborate church structure and service. These Nonconformist sects, as they were called (they did not conform, or agree with, all the teachings of the Anglican Church), stressed the individual's direct relationship with God. All Protestants, but especially Nonconformists, believed that an individual could come to know God through prayer and by reading the Bible. One of the most important outcomes of

A well-dressed congregation leaves a country church after an infant's christening in this 1887 painting by James Charles.

the Reformation was the translation of the Bible into local languages, instead of Latin, across Europe. Since 1611, the King James Bible—the greatest English translation—had been the single most influential book in the English language.

The Anglican Church in the 1800s was torn by factions. So-called High Church advocates stressed spiritualism as expressed in the traditional ceremonies of the church. They tried to beautify Anglican churches by adding elaborate dress, art, and incense, so that worshippers would have a truly elevating religious experience. New churches were built in soaring neo-Gothic splendor.

Broad Church advocates were liberal and tolerant. They tried to emphasize the church's openness to modern science and modern life.

Low Church advocates, called Evangelicals, stressed individual salvation and good works. (Fundamentalist Nonconformists were also called Evangelicals.) Evangelicals were pious and straitlaced. The most fanatical forswore all the pleasures of this life in order to concentrate on the next. Art critic John Ruskin, brought up by strict Evangelical parents, was forbidden to play with toys when he was a child. On Sundays, all the pictures in his house were turned to the wall, and the family ate only cold food.

Many Evangelicals were motivated by a sincere desire to do good. They often turned their zeal for moral reform to humanitarian causes. Most of the social reforms of the nineteenth century were Evangelical in origin: abolishing slavery, public hangings, and flogging; establishing schools; regulating work hours; setting up orphanages and asylums for the poor. Hundreds of charities for every possible social problem were founded, among them the Society for the Prevention of Cruelty to Animals, the Children's Aid Society, the Fresh Air Fund, the Anti-Gambling League, the Young Men's Christian Association, and the Vegetarian Union.

One Sunday in 1902, another national survey was conducted. This time, only 20 percent of the population was in church. Church attendance—and faith—had declined in the sixty-four years of Victoria's reign.

Faith in Crisis

Advances in science and the study of history caused many crises in Victorian faith. Earlier generations could easily believe in the literal truth of the Bible, but thoughtful Victorians often found themselves having to

A VICTORIAN CHRISTMAS

Father Christmas delivers a trayful of goodies in this Victorian Christmas card.

Holly and mistletoe. Fig pudding and steaming hot punch. Christmas cards, Christmas carols, Christmas trees.

Christmas as we know it today is a Victorian creation. Of course, the holiday had been kept in England for centuries, celebrated in church and home with goodwill, good food, and the occasional Yule log. But the sentimentalizing of Christmas was a nineteenth-century phenomenon. So was its commercialization.

Christmas began weeks before December 25, when stores were stocked with toys, books, and knickknacks to entice holiday shoppers. Grocery shelves, and soon larders, were full to bursting with "turkeys, geese, game, poultry, brawn [boar meat], great joints of meat, suckling-pigs, long wreaths of sausages, mince-pies, plum puddings, barrels of oysters, red-hot chestnuts, cherry-cheeked apples, juicy oranges, luscious pears, immense twelfth-cakes, and seething bowls of punch." Working-class families might save their pennies for a whole year to treat themselves to a proper Christmas dinner.

Families decorated their homes with greens, boughs of holly, and clumps of mistletoe. In 1841, Prince Albert set up the first Christmas tree at Windsor Palace, and soon there were trees in parlors across England. The royal children spent hours decorating the tree with German blown-glass ornaments. Families also began to exchange Christmas cards in the 1840s, after the penny post—an inexpensive system for sending mail—was established.

On Christmas Eve, families gathered for carols and games, and on Christmas Day children awoke to stockings full of chocolates, nuts, and oranges. Then came the Christmas dinner, traditionally a goose with applesauce and potatoes, followed by a flaming plum pudding. On Boxing Day, the day after Christmas, those who could afford it distributed money or boxes of used clothes and other goods to the less fortunate.

The greatest all-time promoter of the Victorian Christmas was novelist Charles Dickens. His sentimental vision of Christmas as a time of jollity and humanitarian goodwill is presented in his short novel *A Christmas Carol.* It tells the story of Scrooge, a grouchy, coldhearted miser who is visited by three spirits—the ghosts of Christmas Past, Christmas Present, and Christmas Yet to Come—and becomes kind, cheerful, and generous. "It was always said of him," the story ends, "that he knew how to keep Christmas well, if any man alive possessed the knowledge. May that be truly said of us, and all of us! And so, as Tiny Tim observed, 'God bless, us, Every One!' "

resolve contradictions between the biblical text and recent scholarship. European scholars who studied the Bible found that biblical events did not always fit the historical record. And by studying fossils embedded in rocks, geologists discovered that the earth had been around much longer than the six thousand years the Bible seemed to indicate. Some of the first dinosaur bones discovered, those of an iguanodon in 1822, suggested that an animal had roamed England millions of years ago!

Certainty was further shaken when Charles Darwin published *On the Origin of Species* in 1859. Drawing on compelling scientific evidence,

Nineteenth-century museum visitors view a reconstructed iguanodon skeleton. In the Victorian Age, fossil finds excited great interest in the sciences but also caused anxiety about humankind's place in the natural world.

THE VOYAGE OF THE *BEAGLE*

On December 27, 1831, a young man named Charles Darwin set sail on a voyage that would change his life. The ship HMS *Beagle* traveled to South America on a mission to map the coastline, and Darwin went along to keep the captain company. A brilliant naturalist, he used the voyage to make revolutionary observations of plants and animals.

From every port they reached, Darwin sent back crates of the specimens and fossils he found: the remains of shells, beetles, spiders, and birds, the fossilized bones of prehistoric mammals and dinosaurs. On the barren Galápagos Islands, he made an intriguing discovery. The lizards, tortoises, and birds that lived there were similar to but different from the animals on the South American mainland. Each species differed from island to island, too. Could it be that each variety had developed separately?

After Darwin returned home, it took him more than twenty years to write up and publish his findings. He was worried about the public reaction to his theory. When his book, *On the Origin of Species by means of Natural Selection, or the Preservation of favoured races in the struggle for life* was published in 1859, all 1,250 copies were sold on the first day. As he had feared, there was a public uproar. Yet Charles Darwin never stated that the biblical account of creation was wrong. What he said was that creation did not happen all at once.

New species, Darwin wrote, came about by natural selection. All offspring are different from their parents and from one another. Those that survive the "struggle for existence" are the ones with traits that are best adapted to their environment. On an island with lots of insects, for instance, finches born with long thin beaks will catch more insects than birds with short thick beaks. They will also have more healthy offspring, which in turn will inherit their long thin beaks. On another island, where seeds are the primary food, natural selection will favor finches with short thick beaks. This is how new species develop.

Charles Darwin was a shy man who did not like controversy. But he was fearless in his quest for scientific truth. When he died, he was buried in Westminster Abbey, next to another great British scientist, Sir Isaac Newton.

Darwin advanced the theory that all living things were in a perpetual state of change, or evolution, and that contemporary types of life had evolved from types of life that were now extinct. In short, animals were not created in their final form by one supreme act. Not only that, but humanity itself was not unique. Humans were animals, too—merely in a more advanced stage of evolution.

The doubt and despair felt by many educated Victorians was profound. Each resolved it in his or her own way. Some, like novelist George Eliot, felt compelled to reject the Christian religion while retaining Christian ethics. Some, like critic and writer Thomas Carlyle, experienced a kind of "dark night of the soul" before finding renewed purpose in life and in work. Most found that, even stripped of strict historical accuracy, the Bible still retained an abiding truth and spiritual significance.

Victorian Morality

Victorians believed, above all, in respectability. The term implied good manners, thrift, hard work, neatness, cleanliness, respect for government and the law, and chastity. Today we call these middle-class values. To many of her subjects, Victoria herself was a supreme example of respectability and the role model for her country. "We have come to regard the Crown as the head of our morality," one historian wrote. "We have come to believe that it is natural to have a virtuous sovereign."

At its worst, respectability could mean self-righteousness and Evangelical self-denial. But at its best, the Victorian moral code meant taking responsibility for oneself and for others. It meant putting duty above pleasure—doing what one ought to do before what one wanted to do. Public service was quite as important to many Victorians as private gain—not only at home but abroad. It was typical of the Victorians that, having abolished slavery in their colonies, they spent the next hundred years roaming the seas, trying to abolish the slave trade in the rest of the world. To many—such as Portuguese, African, and Arab traders—the British were interfering busybodies and imperialist aggressors. But the British were convinced they were just doing their duty.

Protestants believed that we are all responsible for our salvation in the next world, and our success in this one. We are all capable of self-improvement through faith, moral action, and above all, hard work. As

Queen Victoria with Albert Edward, the Prince of Wales; Victoria, the Princess Royal; and four more of her nine children, in an idealized portrait. As the queen's family grew, she became the maternal role model for the entire nation.

Thomas Carlyle wrote, "The latest gospel in this world is, 'know thy work and do it.'" The gospel of work as noble and valuable in itself—what we call the Protestant work ethic—led to the energy and commitment of Victorian business. It made possible the rise of England as the world's foremost power.

One of the first self-improvement books ever published was Samuel Smiles's best-selling *Self-Help* (1859). It gave hope to the poor and struggling by preaching that all people could improve their lot in life through discipline and hard work. Victorians trusted in progress—for the nation, the world, *and* the individual.

CHAPTER FOUR

Social Order, Social Change

England in the nineteenth century was a very traditional, ordered society. Yet it was not unalterable, and both social and male/female roles changed considerably as the century went on.

Social Classes

There were at least three distinct classes in Victorian society. For the most part, these were determined not by money but by birth and occupation. Class revealed itself in speech, dress, manners, and education. Everyone was expected to know his or her place on the social ladder, and to maintain it. Members of the lower classes who were copying their "betters" could be accused of "getting above their station." At the same time, members of the upper classes were expected not to "lower themselves."

The working class gained its living by manual labor. Working-class people might work on a farm, in a factory, or as domestic servants in a household. Unskilled laborers usually made just enough money to stay alive. If they lived to an old age, they might have to go to a poorhouse if their children couldn't support them. Skilled laborers, such as carpenters, masons, dressmakers, toolmakers, and bakers, had more money and more opportunities. If they did well, they could educate their children, who might be able to rise in social status to the lower middle class.

The middle classes made up about 25 percent of the population by the end of the Victorian Age. Middle-class people cut a broad swath between laborers and members of the aristocracy (nobility). They were

A flower girl sells her wares outside a London church. This 1888 painting by William Logsdail displays a range of Victorian life: a lower-class street seller, a working-class hackney coach driver, a lower-middle-class mounted policeman (a "bobby"), and an upper-class woman with her daughter.

government workers, military officers, university professors, clergymen, merchants, bankers, industrialists, accountants, journalists, farmers, clerks, and shopkeepers. They educated their children and expected them to succeed through ambition and hard work. It was the middle classes that gave the Victorian Age its distinctive values.

The upper classes included the hereditary landowners. Members of the aristocracy and gentry (landowners who were not nobles) were expected to gain their income through the rental of their property and not to have to work for money. In England in 1842, there were 562 aristocratic families, including dukes, earls, and barons. Then there were hundreds of lesser nobility and a few thousand squires—landed gentlemen with no title. Titles and land were inherited by the eldest son. Younger sons were expected to find work in other professions, such as the military, the church, or the government.

Women

The home was the center of middle-class Victorian life. And the center of the home was the wife and mother. Women occupied a separate sphere, away from the bustling outside world. Once a woman was married, it was understood that she would devote herself full-time to her husband and children. She was the "angel in the house," in the words of a popular poem.

For most of the century, most people thought that women were naturally subservient to men. Few would have disagreed with the sentiments expressed by a character in Tennyson's *The Princess:*

Man for the field and woman for the hearth:
Man for the sword and for the needle she:
Man with the head and woman with the heart:
Man to command and woman to obey;
All else confusion.

The reality was much less ideal. When a woman married, she lost all legal status and property. Man and wife became one person and, as an eminent legal scholar said, "The person is the husband." She could not sue or make a contract or a will. She could not get a divorce, unless she could pay thousands of pounds for an act of Parliament and was willing

VICTORIAN FASHION

Victorian fashion, like the age, was both modest and excessive, sober and silly. The middle-class Victorian male, aiming for a dignified look, typically wore a dark-colored business suit and top hat. By the 1850s, the matched suit of coat, vest, and trousers appeared. In 1846, Elias Howe's sewing machine made mass production possible, ensuring that everyone looked equally respectable.

Female fashions were much more extravagant. Striving for the fashionable waist size of eighteen inches, women wore whalebone corsets, put on in two halves and then laced tightly up the back. For much of the century, women also labored under the weight of five or six layers of petticoats underneath their bell-shaped skirts. At midcentury, the petticoats were replaced by a much lighter "cage crinoline," a circular steel hoop that looked something like a birdcage. Skirts became so enormous that a truly fashionable lady could measure ten yards around at the base. Crinolines were terribly inconvenient. A woman could be knocked over by a sudden gust of wind or catch on fire if her hem came too near the hearth. Even getting through doorways was a challenge.

Women's fashions in 1858. By midcentury, skirts were at their fullest and waistlines at their narrowest. The truly well-dressed lady sported yards of flounces, ribbon, braid, bows, and crocheted trim.

Then suddenly, the bubble burst. From about 1865 on, skirts became progressively narrower. A large padded bustle on the back was all that was left of the great round crinoline. By the century's end, the more independent and active New Woman demanded a freer and more versatile costume. Young women wore knickers (loose-fitting short pants) and a cloth cap to go bicycling and a sporting outfit to play tennis. But corsets did not entirely disappear until World War I ushered in a new generation of girls with bobbed hair and daringly short skirts.

Most women in Victorian England were consumed by household chores, like this countrywoman hanging up the wash while keeping an eye on baby.

to lose her children. The husband was the head of the family and made all its decisions. Ideally, his wife was taken care of for life. But if her husband was violent, broke, unfaithful, or an alcoholic, she had little recourse.

Women who did not marry—and there were many, because there were more women than men in the Victorian Age—had few options. For most of the century, the only occupations open to middle-class women were teaching and governessing—both low-status, low-income jobs.

Working-class women were never expected to be household angels. In factories and home industries, they were the most exploited of workers, except for children. Many a single woman or widow with children ruined her health and eyesight hand-tinting illustrations, making boxes, or plaiting straw for hats by candlelight.

The movement for women's rights gained momentum as the century progressed, despite Conservative opposition. Ever the traditionalist, Victoria wrote, "The Queen is most anxious to enlist everyone who can speak or write to join in checking this mad wicked folly of women's Rights, with all its attendant horrors, on which her poor feeble sex is bent, forgetting every sense of womanly feeling and propriety."

Nonetheless, eventually laws were changed to allow women to keep their own property when they married, to keep custody of their children in the event of separation, and to obtain a divorce. The Victorian "New Women" of the 1880s and 1890s found themselves working in shops and offices as secretaries, typists, telephone operators, librarians, bookkeepers, nurses, and in a host of other professions.

Children and Education

Children were much loved in Victorian times, but they led precarious lives. Even in upper-class households, infant mortality was high—more than one in ten—throughout the period. None of the inoculations we have today against the so-called childhood diseases yet existed. In addition, children were vulnerable to tuberculosis and epidemics of cholera, typhoid, and diphtheria. But smallpox was gradually eliminated in the century, and better sewage treatment and drainage helped reduce the death rate. Between 1875 and the end of the century, life expectancy rose from forty to forty-four for men and from forty-two to forty-eight for women.

The average household included six children in 1850, although many upper-class households had as many as ten. Children of different social classes led very different lives. In the upper classes, children lived an almost entirely separate existence from their parents. Their full-time caretaker was a nanny, who lived with them in the "nursery" on the upper floor of the home. In middle-class homes, a nursery maid, usually a young girl, watched over the children, and the mother helped out with teaching and minding. Parents spent more time with their children and even ate some meals with them. In working-class homes, the oldest girl of the family generally took care of the other children. An eight-year-old girl might have full responsibility for a toddler.

IF YOU LIVED IN VICTORIAN ENGLAND

If you had been born in 1840 during the reign of Queen Victoria, your way of life would have been determined by the facts of your birth—whether you were a girl or a boy; wealthy or poor; upper, middle, or working class. With this chart you can trace the course your life might have taken if you were a member of an upper-middle-class family.

You were born in Oxford. . . .

As a Boy . . . / **As a Girl . . .**

You live with your parents in a comfortable home on the banks of the Cherwell River. Your father is a doctor with a prosperous practice in the university town. From the nursery window, you can see students rowing on the river. Although you take meals with your nursery maid, you spend a lot of time with your parents and older siblings.

As a Boy

At age 5 you are educated at home by a governess, who teaches you arithmetic and your ABCs. On Sundays you attend the local Church of England services with your family, where you learn to read your first prayers. You love to ride your family's pony.

At age 8 you leave home to attend a public boarding school. There you learn to read and translate Greek and Latin classics such as Virgil's *Aeneid* and study a few modern subjects, including mathematics, science, and history. Every holiday you come home to visit your family.

At age 16 you begin studying the law and modern history at the university. At 19 you take the foreign service examinations and go abroad to India. There you begin your career in colonial administration and learn to play polo.

At age 27 you marry while on home leave in England. You and your wife return to India, where you raise a family and join the local cricket club and Anglican church. After 20 years you retire to a comfortable house in Oxford. There you write your memoirs on your life in India and write articles for the local historical society.

As a Girl

At age 5 you are taught arithmetic and your ABCs by a governess. Your mother begins to teach you how to sew. On Sundays you go to church with your family and learn to read the prayers. You love to ride the family's pony.

At age 8 you continue your studies with your governess, learning English, history, geography, and French. As you get older, you have drawing and dancing masters and a piano teacher as well. In the summers you visit a seaside resort with your family.

At age 16 you go away to a boarding school to learn the social graces and improve your French. After graduation you spend six months on the European continent with a friend and her family. In your twenties you live at home with your family, helping your mother run the household and attending social events. You often take the train into London for the day, where you enjoy visiting art galleries and going to the theater.

At age 25 you marry the rector of a local church and begin raising a family. Your husband provides a comfortable living and you are able to educate your seven children. You join the local garden club and enjoy organizing yearly church festivals for the village.

In old age you are taken care of by your children and grandchildren. You enjoy some of the new conveniences of modern life, such as telephones and automobiles, but are dismayed by the relaxed dress and manners of the younger generation. When you die, you are buried in the graveyard of the local Anglican church in a traditional ceremony.

Children at play in a Victorian village

Children had always worked, usually in agriculture or in cottage (home) industries with their parents or other relatives. But the Industrial Revolution meant that for the first time large numbers of children were working away from home under the supervision of a business owner or overseer. Parliament began to intervene on behalf of children, setting standards for hours and ages. By the end of the nineteenth century, few children under twelve could be employed anywhere (although many still worked at home doing sewing and other crafts). But more than half of the children over twelve were still working, in factories or farms, or as domestic servants, indentured apprentices, or office boys.

Education improved by fits and starts throughout the century. In the 1830s, families of means might have a governess for their daughters, and a tutor might educate a son until he left for a public boarding school or university. Most middle-class children had to make do with "dame schools"—local schools taught by women of limited knowledge and ability. Working-class children might learn their ABCs in Sunday school, in order to read the Bible.

As the century went on, "national" schools were founded, partially funded by the government. As many as five hundred boys and girls would be taught by three teachers and twelve pupil teachers, or monitors. Not surprisingly, most of the education was mere memorization. After the Education Acts of 1870 and 1880, which made education compulsory (required), classes became a bit smaller and all schools taught the same subjects.

For middle-class boys, there were also day schools and boarding schools. And for boys of prosperous middle- and upper-class families, there were the famous "public" schools such as Eton and Harrow. There, for most of the century, boys were taught primarily Greek and Latin. Only some went on to university at Oxford or Cambridge. Getting a college education was not yet necessary for success.

Girls' education was much more haphazard. Since they were not expected to make a living, girls from well-to-do families might be taught by a governess,

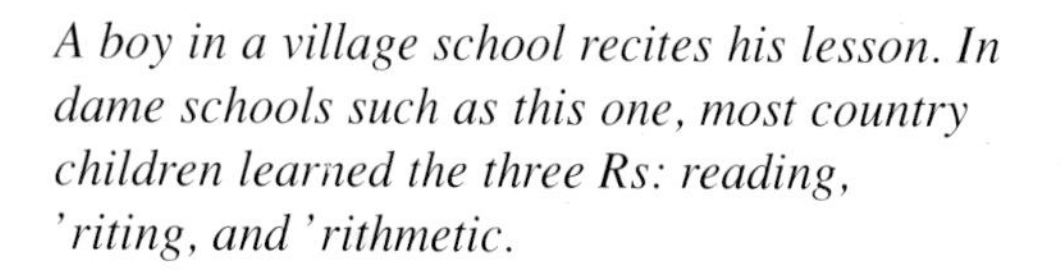

A boy in a village school recites his lesson. In dame schools such as this one, most country children learned the three Rs: reading, 'riting, and 'rithmetic.

sometimes sharing one with another family. Some girls went to a nearby day school. When they got older, they might go to a boarding school, where the emphasis was usually on social accomplishments, with a smattering of academic subjects. University was not available to girls until the last quarter of the century, and few took advantage of the opportunity. Working-class girls, like their brothers, might go to elementary school for a few years, although their time there was usually limited because their help was needed at home. By the end of the century, there was more and better education for girls of all classes.

CHAPTER FIVE

A Lasting Memory

In 1851, the year of the Crystal Palace Exhibition, a young German was studying in the reading room of the British Museum in London. His name was Karl Marx (1818–1883), and he had been expelled from Germany as a dangerous revolutionary. Like other European radicals, he settled in England, where a tradition of intellectual freedom allowed him to write without interference. Marx was writing *Das Kapital* (1867), the book that would give birth to communism and inspire the Russian Revolution.

Even at the height of the age, forces were at work to change the Victorian way of life forever.

The Passing of an Age

The crowd that gathered for Victoria's funeral in 1901 included most of the crowned heads of Europe—grand dukes and kings and tsars and kaisers from Germany, Spain, Russia, Sweden, Denmark, Romania. Within thirteen years, Europe would be engulfed by the horrors of World War I (1914–1918) and most monarchies would be blown to rubble, never to return. The British royal house, however, would endure. Victoria and Albert had fashioned a modern monarchy that was above politics. It would help keep the British identity intact into the twenty-first century, through two world wars and the loss of the empire.

Although the monarchy remained, the Victorian spirit would disappear. After the war, members of the younger generation discussed socialism and psychology. They smoked, drank, danced the Charleston, drove fast cars—and ridiculed their grandparents' code of respectability. To young people, Victorianism meant insincerity and narrow-mindedness. For the first decades of the twentieth century, even Victorian literature and art were disdained as fussy, moralistic, and ridiculously unmodern.

Crowds line the streets for Queen Victoria's funeral procession, February 2, 1901. To honor the queen, London's streets were draped with purple hangings and white satin bows.

The End of Imperialism

Anti-imperialist sentiment grew in the first decades of the twentieth century. Slowly but surely, Britain lost its colonies. The first to go were those that had been heavily settled by the British. Canada became independent in 1867, Australia in 1901, New Zealand in 1907, and South Africa in 1909. These former colonies remained part of the empire, becoming dominions—self-governing nations that still recognized the British monarch as head of state.

Queen Elizabeth II officially opens the 1992 Parliament. The British monarchy has endured to the present day, thanks in large part to Queen Victoria's understanding of the limited role of the monarch in a constitutional government.

The issue of Home Rule for Ireland continued to trouble the British Isles into the twentieth century. By World War I, radicals in a group later known as the Irish Republican Army (IRA) were staging guerrilla attacks against the British army and police. In 1921, the Anglo-Irish Treaty formally recognized the existence of the independent Irish Free State (now known as the Republic of Ireland) in southern Ireland. But the six mainly

Protestant counties of Ulster in the northeast remained part of the United Kingdom, as Northern Ireland. From the 1960s on, a bitter terrorist war has raged between the IRA and Ulster Protestants. Although numerous peace attempts have been made, by the twenty-first century no lasting truce had been reached.

In India, the independence movement that had begun with the Indian Mutiny in 1857 continued with the founding of the first Indian National Congress in 1885. When Indian nationalism began to gather momentum, before and after World War I, the British realized they should prepare for withdrawal. Already there was a class of university-educated Indians working in law, the government, and the civil service. Railways and telegraph lines crisscrossed the country. As a result, India already had the makings of a modern state when it became independent in 1947. Today India is the largest democracy in the world. Like many of the former British colonies, it is a member of the Commonwealth of Nations—a voluntary association of more than fifty nations with close ties to Britain.

Other British colonies to achieve self-rule after World War II, such as Singapore and Jamaica, also made a successful transition to self-government. The former African colonies, hampered by the poverty and tribal conflicts of their continent, have had a rougher road. And that bane of the Victorian Evangelicals, slavery, still exists in places such as the Sudan, where General Gordon made his final stand in the siege of Khartoum.

The Return of Victorianism

Queen Victoria died a mere hundred years ago. The century since then has brought horrors of genocide and terrorism as well as technological triumphs that would have been inconceivable to her or to any of her subjects. Now we are able to look back on the nineteenth century clearly and from a distance. We know we have no right to feel superior.

Victorian art has become fashionable again. Narrative paintings fetch high prices at auction houses, overpadded sofas and ornately carved furniture fill the antique stores, and William Morris prints come to second life in carpets and fabrics and wallpaper. Victorian novels, still read and loved after all these years, undergo new transformations on TV and in the movies. We hum along to the music of *Oliver!* and thrill to the ghosts of *Scrooge*.

THE NEW ENGLISHES

The most lasting legacy of the British Empire may well be the globalization of the English language. It is an official language in some thirty-four countries on six continents, from Singapore and India to Sierra Leone and South Africa to Jamaica and Canada. What we call "standard English" is the international language of trade and diplomacy. But there are many other "Englishes" as well.

Wherever it was planted, English has borne different fruit. In Jamaica, the local Creole is a simplified English that retains the grammatical structure of the languages slaves brought with them from Africa. Krio, in West Africa, mixes English, Yoruba, Portuguese, and French. The English word *man* can find many different meanings in Krio: *man klos* (man's dress), *man pawa* (man power, or strength), *manpus* (man puss, or tomcat). Nonstandard English in Singapore, called "Singlish," is influenced by Chinese, Malay, and Tamil.

The English language has been spoken in India for more than two hundred years, and there may be more speakers of different varieties of English there than in Britain. The Victorians themselves borrowed many words from the Indians: *bandanna, jungle, curry, veranda, bungalow.* English rule in India created a basically bilingual society. Today Indian writers have made Indian English an internationally recognized language, an English all its own.

We light our Christmas trees every year.

We owe an enormous amount to the Victorians, both good and bad. What can we say about an age that gave us railroads, afternoon tea, anesthetics, the yellow pencil, the postage stamp, canned food, the Boy Scouts, factories, antislavery laws, Charles Dickens, Lewis Carroll, and the umbrella?

The Christmas tree at Rockefeller Center, New York. Many of our cherished Christmas traditions came from the Victorians.

For all its contradictions, the Victorian Age will be remembered as one of the most influential and creative periods in human history—a time when not just a sovereign, but a whole people, tried to "be good." They didn't always succeed, but the example of their vigor and determination lives on.

Victorian England: A Time Line

1769 | **1800**

1769 James Watt gets patent for improved steam engine

1801 Act of Union creates the United Kingdom of Great Britain and Ireland

1815 Napoleonic Wars end

1819 Victoria born

1832 First Reform Bill passes

1834 Slavery abolished throughout the British Empire

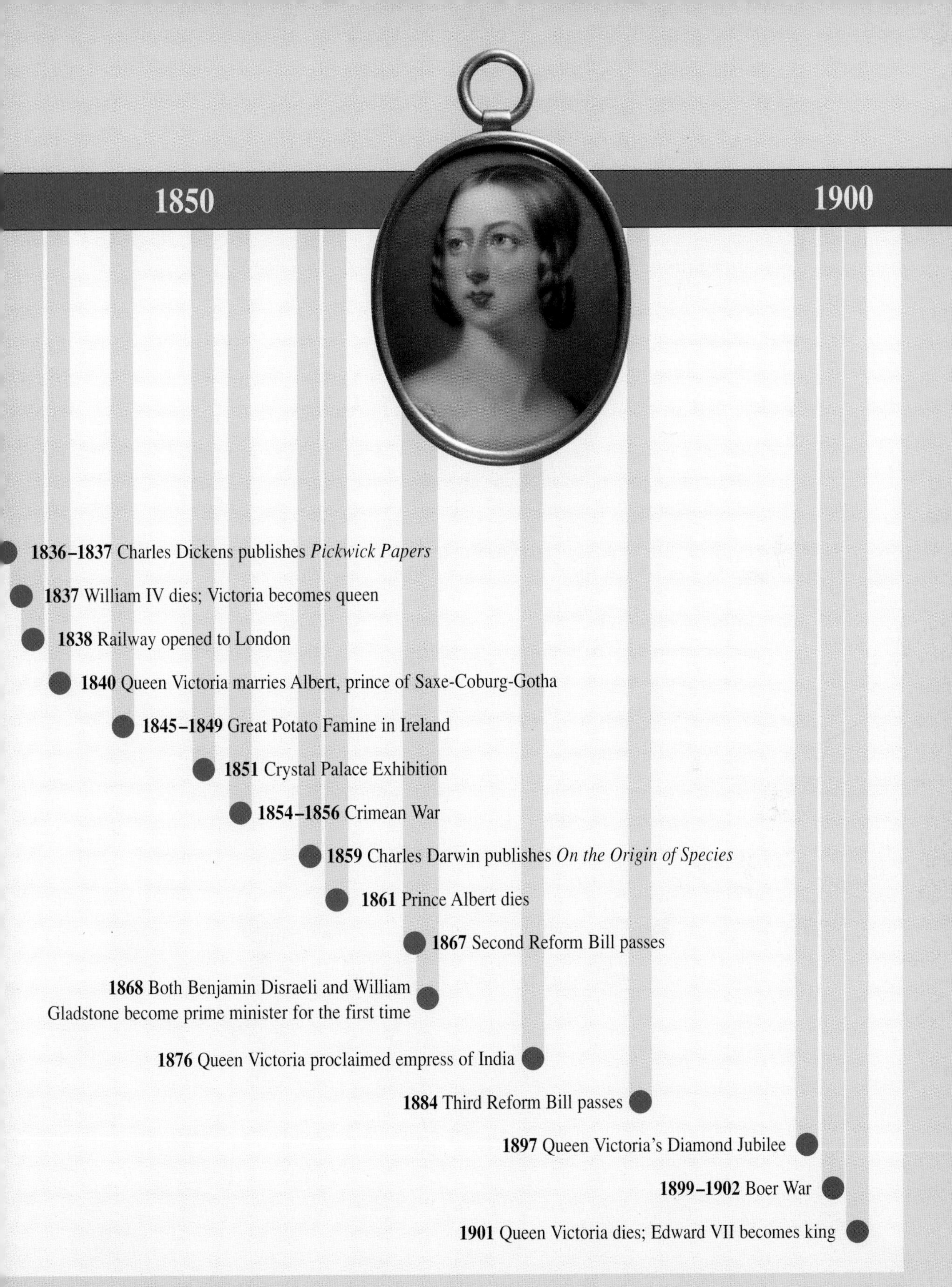

1836–1837 Charles Dickens publishes *Pickwick Papers*

1837 William IV dies; Victoria becomes queen

1838 Railway opened to London

1840 Queen Victoria marries Albert, prince of Saxe-Coburg-Gotha

1845–1849 Great Potato Famine in Ireland

1851 Crystal Palace Exhibition

1854–1856 Crimean War

1859 Charles Darwin publishes *On the Origin of Species*

1861 Prince Albert dies

1867 Second Reform Bill passes

1868 Both Benjamin Disraeli and William Gladstone become prime minister for the first time

1876 Queen Victoria proclaimed empress of India

1884 Third Reform Bill passes

1897 Queen Victoria's Diamond Jubilee

1899–1902 Boer War

1901 Queen Victoria dies; Edward VII becomes king

GLOSSARY

Anglican Church: the established Church of England, founded by King Henry VIII in 1534

Anglo–Saxons: a Germanic people who conquered Britain in the fifth century

cavalry: the part of an army that is mounted on horseback

classical: pertaining to the ancient Greeks and Romans; in music, the European tradition that includes choral music, chamber music, and orchestral music

Conservative (Tory) party: a British political party emphasizing tradition and social stability

constitutional monarchy: a government headed by a king, queen, or other monarch whose power is limited by law and by an elected body of representatives

entrepreneur: someone who starts, manages, and takes on the financial risks of a new business

Evangelical: a Protestant who believes in salvation through faith and in the literal truth of the Bible

genocide: the deliberate destruction of a racial, political, or cultural group of people

gentry: a landowning class below the nobility and above the middle class

guerrilla: a type of warfare carried out by independent bands who engage in harassment and sabotage

hierarchy: the leaders of a church, organized into ranks

Hindu: a follower of Hinduism, the main religion of India

imperialism: the policy of extending the power of a country by taking over or politically influencing other territories

indentured: bound by a contract to work for another person for a period of time in order to learn a trade

Industrial Revolution: the introduction of power-driven machinery in Europe and the United States in the late eighteenth and early nineteenth centuries, and the changes in society that resulted

laissez-faire economics: a policy that opposes government interference in economic affairs

Liberal (Whig) party: a British political party emphasizing individual freedom and reform

Muslim: a follower of the faith of Islam, founded by the prophet Muhammad in the early seventh century

naturalist: someone who studies the natural development of plants or animals

Nonconformist: a British Protestant who does not follow the doctrines of the Anglican Church

nostalgia: a sentimental attachment to the past

Parliament: the legislative body of British government

pound: the basic monetary unit of the United Kingdom

Pre-Raphaelites: a brotherhood of artists founded in England in 1848 to revive the simple, beautiful style of Italian painters before Raphael

propriety: a standard of proper social behavior

protagonist: the main character of a story

Protestant Reformation: the revolution within the Roman Catholic Church in Europe in the sixteenth century that led to the establishment of Protestantism

Raj: the British rule in India

republic: a form of government in which citizens vote for elected representatives

Romanticism: a literary, artistic, and philosophical movement starting in the late eighteenth century that emphasized the power of the imagination and the importance of individual experience

suffrage: the right to vote

FOR FURTHER READING

Anderson, Margaret J. *Charles Darwin: Naturalist.* Hillside, NJ: Enslow, 1994.

Bartoletti, Susan Campbell. *Black Potatoes: The Story of the Great Irish Famine, 1845–1850.* Boston: Houghton Mifflin, 2001.

Brontë, Charlotte. *Jane Eyre.* New York: Grosset and Dunlap, 2000.

Carroll, Lewis. *Alice's Adventures in Wonderland.* New York: Dover, 1993.

Corrick, James A. *The Industrial Revolution.* San Diego: Lucent Books, 1998.

Dickens, Charles. *A Christmas Carol.* New York: Viking, 2000.

———. *Oliver Twist.* New York: Puffin Books, 1994.

Gallagher, Carol. *The Irish Potato Famine.* New York: Chelsea House, 2001.

Kirwan, Anna. *Victoria: May Blossom of Britannia.* New York: Scholastic, 2001.

Myers, Walter Dean. *At Her Majesty's Request: An African Princess in Victorian England.* New York: Scholastic, 1999.

Shearman, Deirdre. *Queen Victoria.* New York: Chelsea House, 1986.

Stanley, Diane, and Peter Vennema. *Charles Dickens: The Man Who Had Great Expectations.* New York: Morrow Junior Books, 1993.

Stevenson, Robert Louis. *Treasure Island.* New York: Viking, 1996.

Swisher, Clarice. *Victorian England.* San Diego: Lucent Books, 2001.

Ventura, Piero. *Darwin: Nature Reinterpreted.* Boston: Houghton Mifflin, 1995.

ON-LINE INFORMATION*

"1875 Victorian England Revisited" at http://www.logicmgmt.com/1876/splash.htm

Travel back in time to Victorian England and experience middle-class life as it was then.

"Ironbridge Gorge Museums" at http://www.ironbridge.org.uk

Take a virtual tour of Coalbrookdale in Shropshire, England, the "birthplace of the Industrial Revolution."

"The Victorian Web" at http://65.107.211.206/victor.html

This is perhaps the most comprehensive site on Victorian England, with links to pages on history, science, technology, religion, authors, and many other topics.

*Websites change from time to time. For additional on-line information, check with the media specialist at your local library.

BIBLIOGRAPHY

Adams, Robert M. *The Land and Literature of England.* New York: Norton, 1983.

Altick, Richard D. *Victorian People and Ideas.* New York: Norton, 1973.

Best, Geoffrey. *Mid-Victorian Britain, 1851–75.* New York: Schocken Books, 1972.

Briggs, Asa. *A Social History of England.* London: Weidenfeld and Nicolson, 1994.

Chiflet, Jean-Loup, and Alain Beaulet. *Victoria and Her Times.* New York: Henry Holt, 1996.

Gascoigne, Bamber. *Encyclopedia of Britain.* London: MacMillan, 1994.

Gaunt, William. *The Restless Century: Painting in Britain 1800–1900.* Oxford, England: Phaidon, 1972.

Huttenback, Robert A. *The British Imperial Experience.* New York: Harper and Row, 1966.

Johnson, Edgar. *Charles Dickens: His Tragedy and Triumph.* New York: Viking Press, 1977.

Kemper, Rachel H. *A History of Costume.* New York: Newsweek Books, 1977.

Longford, Elizabeth. *Queen Victoria: Born to Succeed.* New York: Harper & Row, 1964.

McCrum, Robert, William Cran, and Robert MacNeil. *The Story of English.* New York: Penguin Books, 1986.

Mitchell, Sally. *Daily Life in Victorian England.* Westport, CT: Greenwood Press, 1996.

Pool, Daniel. *What Jane Austen Ate and Charles Dickens Knew.* New York: Simon and Schuster, 1993.

Wilson, A. N. *Eminent Victorians.* New York: W. W. Norton, 1989.

INDEX

Page numbers for illustrations are in boldface

About the Author

Ruth Ashby was educated at Yale University and the University of Virginia, where she studied Victorian literature and culture. Ever since reading *Jane Eyre* and *Oliver Twist* at age ten, she has longed to live in the England of Charlotte Brontë and Charles Dickens. She has written more than twenty nonfiction books for young people, including *Elizabethan England* (Benchmark Books 1999), *Around the World in 1800* (Benchmark Books 2003) and *Herstory* (Viking 1995). She hopes to write many more.